TIME ALONE

Alessandro Camon

BROADWAY PLAY PUBLISHING INC
New York
www.broadwayplaypub.com
info@broadwayplaypub.com

TIME ALONE
© Copyright 2019 Alessandro Camon

Cover art by Mark Jackson/Properly Creative,
    courtesy of Belle Rêve Theatre Company
First edition: January 2019
I S B N: 978-0-88145-823-7
Book design: Marie Donovan
Page make-up: Adobe InDesign
Typeface: Palatino

TIME ALONE was given its world premiere by the Belle Rêve Theatre Company at the Los Angeles Theatre Center in September 2017. The cast and creative contributors were:

GABRIEL WAYLAND.................................Alex Hernandez
ANNA JACKSON .... Tonya Pinkins

Director...Bart De Lorenzo
Set design............................... Francois-Pierre Couture
Costume design...Ingrid Ferrin
Lighting design........................Pablo Santiago-Brandwein
Sound design.. John Zalewski
Projection design...Keith Skretch

The production received The Los Angeles Drama Critics Circle Ted Schmitt Award for World Premiere, of an Outstanding New Play and the Lead Performance Award for Tonya Pinkins. It also received the Stage Raw Awards for Playwriting and Two-Person Performance, and was nominated for five Ovation Awards.

In 2018, Bonnie Franklin Classic and Contemporary American Plays Series produced a series of staged readings in Los Angeles and Chicago. They were directed by Sal Lopez, and featured Richard Cabral, Alex Fernandez, Xavi Moreno, Hattie Winston, and Lisa Gay Hamilton.

THANKS

This story is a work of fiction, but it's informed by hundreds of people I met inside and outside California's prisons and juvenile halls. I wish to thank them, and every teacher, advocate, and activist who works toward decarceration and criminal justice reform.

I'm particularly grateful to the Anti-Recidivism Coalition, Scott Budnick and Jose Gonzales—who opened many doors for me, literally and figuratively.

In addition, I'd like to thank Michelle Nunez and Tanya Cohen at Belle Reve Theatre and everyone who worked on the original production, as well as the 2018 staged reading series, plus Jay Rodan, Tara Summers, and Kayt Jones for their help and support.

And most of all: Suzanne Warren—wife, partner, producer, editor, navigator, bullshit detector, and constant inspiration.

CHARACTERS

GABRIEL WAYLAND *is 34 years old, Hispanic/Caucasian. He's serving a 50-to-life sentence for the murder of a rival gang member. He spent 5 years in solitary confinement. He was born in Los Angeles. His Hispanic inflection is acquired, and can be dialed up or down. He is street-raised, self-educated, sharp, charismatic. He has a muscular build, shuffling gait, and vigilant, restless eyes. He shifts, sometimes abruptly, from calm and still to hyper.*

ANNA JACKSON *is 53, African-American, the mother of a police officer killed in the line of duty. She is originally from Texas, and speaks with a Southern accent. She relocated to Northern California after her son's death. She currently works part-time as a notary public and a private student tutor to supplement her survivor benefits. Anna is fiercely intelligent, intense, broken and yet forceful. Her appetite for life has been suppressed by trauma, rather than dimmed by age.*

PRODUCTION

The play alternates between the two characters, who speak from opposite sides of the stage. On one side is GABRIEL's *single-occupancy, level 4 (highest security) prison cell, with no window. It has a cement shelf for a bed, small built-in cubicle for a mini-desk, small built-in stool, and a metal toilet-sink combo unit. On the other side is Anna's spare, tidy kitchen, which has old-fashioned appliances, a window, and a table with three chairs. Both characters will sit, stand or pace as desired.*

If imagery or sound effects are deployed, they should be stylized and evocative, rather than function as literal reenactment. Overall, the play should have an intimate, confessional quality.

Importantly, the characters are not in a dialogue; they address the audience, rather than one another. Their tales are intersecting monologues spoken from different places. While one is speaking, the other should not appear to be listening. At any given point, the non-speaking character might be engaged in simple activities (exercising, cleaning, eating, reading, etc.), or disappear altogether in darkness.

GABRIEL: You're gonna have to bear with me.
I don't do this too much.
I mean, talk to people. Regular people.
You know…*free* people.

I should start with my name.
I got one of those you can say two ways:
Gay-bree-uhl—
Gah-bryel—
I use either. Depends who I'm talking to.
Last name's Wayland.
My mom never changed it.

One day, we're riding the bus,
I ask her: Why do we keep his name?
He's been gone three years—
He's never coming back—
Hell, *we don't want him back.*

She says:
My *first* husband was worse.
My father, don't get me started.
You think I miss their names?

So, there you go:
Gabriel Jessie Wayland.
I mostly grew up with my mom,
My brother and my sister.
My mom had problems—
Money problems
Men problems
Drug problems
Sooner or later, they all became *our* problems.

There's this Clint Eastwood movie,
Escape from Alcatraz...
In the movie, this dude asks him:
How was your childhood?
And Clint answers:
Short.

That's it, right there:
Short.
Says it all in one word.
Kind of a perfect word,
'Cause the word *short* is short...
Though, come to think of it,
It's longer than the word *long.*
And shorter than the word *shorter.*

Whatever. I like that line.
I could say the same.
Tell me, Gabriel:
How was your childhood?
Short.

But now I got time. Right?
I can tell you the longer story.
So picture this—
I'm nine years old.
Don't know how to swim
Never seen snow
Never gone out of town
Shit, I barely ever left the hood.
One day, I'm hanging out on the street
I hear the shots
POP POP POP
Then see the car drive away
And there it is:

My first dead body.
Brain matter on the sidewalk.
I don't know that's what it's called.

Brain matter.
But I know about murders.
So I don't freak out.
I know people get shot.

I take a long look at the body,
Before someone tells me, *get the fuck home.*

I see more dead bodies after that.
A dolphin
Or an elephant—
I've only seen those on T V.

My father, he has a nickname for me.
He calls me 40 Bucks.
I'm kind of flattered—
I mean, it ain't a million
But it ain't a penny, either.
To me, it's a fortune.
And he says it with a smile.
it sounds cool
I'm cool with it
I don't like it when my mom tells him to stop.
Let the man call me 40 Bucks, for fuck's sake.
But he listens to her, and he stops.

After he leaves us,
My mom tells us we'll be fine
We're still a family
Uncle Bennie's gonna help.

Uncle Bennie lives with his girlfriend and a dog.
His favorite joke is, he don't know which is which.
My uncle gets drunk, and watches porn.
One day he starts showing me
I'm like ten years old
I don't want to see this—
I mean, what the fuck.
He laughs at me and tells me I'm dumb.
Tells me: *this is what men do.*

It's not like my friends have it better.
The girls—
They have it worse—
By the time they're sixteen
Half of them have been raped.
I hear the stories from my sister.

She doesn't tell me *her* story.
The one about uncle Bennie.
I hear that years later,
After he's already dead.

Ivan would have protected her.
(Note: he pronounces it: ee-vahn.)

Ivan's our big brother.
Four years older than me.
Different father—His was named Estrada.
Died when Ivan was two.

Ivan's tough. Straight-up gangster.
But at the time he's in jail for burglary,
So he knows nothing about uncle Bennie—
Nothing he could do about it, anyhow.

I'm like, thirteen.
Ivan's gonna be inside a while.
He's gonna grow out of his clothes
So now I get to wear 'em.
I don't mind that—
He's got some cool clothes.
And I want to be cool—
I want to be just like him.
When he tells me: Don't follow my footsteps,
All I can think is: *I like his shoes.*

That year, I decide to get my nickname back.
I'm gonna make it my street name.
I'm gonna be *40 Bucks.*
Now, street names,
You don't get to pick your own

So I gotta be slick about this.
I start small.
Just a few friends.
Little by little, it begins to catch.

And that's when my mom finds out—
She goes,
You dumb little shit
You know why he called you that?
I say, 'cause he liked me.
She says, *Abortion*.
I don't understand.

She says, When we went to the clinic,
We were forty bucks short
So we said fuck it, we'll keep it
We called you 40 Bucks
Before we ever called you Gabriel.

A few weeks later, I'm with my friends,
I say something random about China.
How it'd be cool to see the Great Wall.
When this guy calls me *dreamy*
I pretend to be annoyed—
What the fuck did you call me?
He says, dreamy
I called you dreamy
'Cause you always be having dreams and shit.
I say, don't fucking call me dreamy,
And then of course they all do—
Dreamy becomes my street name.

I spend all my time in the street.
The homies show me love.
Hook me up with food, weed, girls
And I'm *proud* of protecting our streets—
Like my brother did
Like all the big homies did
We're like child soldiers

Like those African kids
Except they got kidnapped
We were *born* into this.

I got good memories
Playing soccer in the park
Until it's too dark to see the ball

Riding my bike
Breeze spreading the smells
Jasmine, jacaranda
Meat sizzling in the taco trucks

Girls in tight jeans
short-cropped tops
Tattoos peeking out
Lips like berries

My brother sharing stolen chocolate
And good Alaskan weed...

I remember.

(A pause)

So, anyway...
Eventually, my mom leaves with a man.
After a week, she calls to say
She had to go out of town.
She's not sure how long.
She gives me some bullshit story
I know right then it's bullshit
Thing is, she didn't pay rent before leaving
So we get kicked out.

I end up sleeping on grandma's couch
In the church basement
In a condemned office building

All I got is my homies
We take care of each other
We do what we gotta do to survive.

And then, one day, this kid
Ramon Santos
He's with a bunch of fools
Who kick it a few blocks down
They come around to our street
They start tagging
Linda sees them from her window

Linda— She's tough...
I used to call her my girlfriend,
'Cause she let me do stuff when we were thirteen.
But then she said:
I'm not your girlfriend
I just gave you a free ride
Don't go make a big thing out of it...

Anyway, Linda—
She gets all up in their grill—
Fuck you think you are
Tagging our hood
Disrespecting us like that.
Ramon calls her a bitch
She calls him a punk
He whips out his gun and shoots her.

She's in the hospital—
May or may not live.
This older homie says,
We gonna do something about it.
He's high
We're all high
He tells me, *It's your turn*
You're due for your heart-check
I ask, What d'you want me to do?
He says, You know what—
You gonna *smoke* that fool
Gonna put up some tape
In *their* motherfucking hood...

Man, I knew this day was coming.
I got my cholo down,
But truth is, I'm half and half
Pocho
Guero
Rice and beans
Cafe con leche
I'm Dreamy
Ivan's little brother
Long story, short:
I gotta prove myself.

We smoke more meth before we go.
Tito's driving. I sit next to him.
Tweeks and Hefty in the back.
We get to the house.
Ramon's out front.
There's loud music.
He doesn't hear us coming.
I hear the words inside my head
Gotta smoke that fool
Gotta put up some tape

I walk over—
I squeeze the trigger…

And that's it.
He goes down. I run.
I never even see his eyes.

Three days later Tito's arrested.
By evening he's made a deal.
Fingers me up as the shooter
Takes the rap as an accessory
Gets bonus points for snitching.

They offer me a plea.
Twenty-five years.
Lawyer says don't take it
Which is unusual

But I figure he knows what he's doing.
Better tried by twelve
Than carried by six
That's what they say in the hood.

I'm just shy of eighteen
I get tried as an adult.
And now get this:
They say we can't talk
About what Ramon did.
They say it's not proven
And he's not the one on trial.

They show pictures of him in a school uniform.
Smiling
Big eyes
Those eyes I'd never seen before
Then they show a crime scene photo
The eyes are still open
A witness says he pulled down the lids
But they rolled right back up.
Something happens after that.
I go to sleep at night
It's like this trick in my head—
I'm closing my eyes,
And I see his flip open
These big dead eyes
Staring at me.

Linda lives.
She tells people she's not sure who shot her.
Maybe she's scared.
Doesn't matter.
I want him to be guilty,
But deep inside, *I know*...
I know that whether he did it or not
He was a kid like me
Scared, and high
And alone, and stupid.

The trial's quick.
Day and a half.
The foreman stands up,
And in this whiny voice he says:
We find the defendant guilty.

Later, they add the enhancements
Gotta love that word
Like they're making this better
Firearm
Gang-related
Each enhancement is another stretch
Total's fifty-to-life
My lawyer cost me an extra twenty-five.
It's like that old prison joke:
For a good time, call a hooker
For a long time, call my lawyer.

When I hear it, fifty to life,
I know what it means—I just can't feel it.
They might as well have said five hundred.
It's like something from a movie—
A long time ago...
The far, far future...
It's dinosaur time
Space travel time
I've only been alive seventeen years
I never even went to Chuck E Cheese.

You believe that?
I've never even been to Chuck E Cheese.

(ANNA *extracts a plate of food from a microwave oven. She picks at it. A couple of bites, then she pushes the plate away. After a moment:*)

ANNA: I used to cook.
I *loved* to cook.
It's a simple thing, when you break it down to basics:

It comes down to heat and time.
But then again, there are many ways
You can combine heat and time.
You can boil, bake, sear, fry.
You can roast, poach, char, flambé…
You get my point.
You need to have a plan.
And you need to have a feel for it.

I always did. I had a feel for it,
And I liked that sense of accomplishing something.
Most days, you work all day,
And you never actually finish a thing.
You're not really *making* anything, anyway.
But then you go home,
And you can make a chicken pie from scratch,
And you can eat it with someone you love.

And that used to be my life.

My name is Anna Jackson.
Jackson is my married name.
I met my husband, Carl,
When we were in the same high school.
He was one year older,
But his class was next door,
So I saw him all the time.
I felt something for him right away.
I thought he felt something for me—
But he had a girlfriend—In fact, he had a few.
This, too, I guess, comes down to heat and time—
And I guess that wasn't our time.

A few years later, I'm working in a law office—
I'm a floating assistant, bottom of the totem pole.
One day, I'm bringing some papers to the courthouse,
When I leave I see Carl outside.
He's in uniform. He's a cop now.
It was always his dream --

He wanted to help the community,
And not from behind a desk—
He wanted to be out there, with people.
He was always that guy
The guy who chats up strangers at the checkout line,
Who offers to carry your bag,
The guy with the easy smile...

When I see him, he looks overjoyed
And I look at that smile,
And something inside me shakes loose—
It's like my body knows,
And my mind's playing catch up.
I guess it's about, what d'you call it—
Neurochemistry, I think.

He asks me, *You like coffee?*
I say, I *love* coffee—And not the weak stuff either—
I don't want no coffee
That you can see the world through—
Give me some dark, strong coffee,
Sweet as love and hot as hell—
And damn if I'm not already flirting with him.

He says his shift just ended,
And he knows a coffeeshop, three blocks away,
Makes the best coffee in the world—
And the sandwiches are great, too.

My lunch break is about to start,
So I follow him to the coffeeshop.
We stay for an hour.
By the end of the week we're sleeping together.
By the end of the month he moves in with me.
My mother starts asking
If we have a wedding date in mind.
She says, mothers know these things.

One day we go to the beach.
He has a bracelet I haven't seen before.

I ask him about it.
He says his old girlfriend gave it to him.
I know he's trying to make me jealous.
I ask him if I can see it.
It's a nice bracelet,
And I say, *Nice bracelet*—
And I just throw it into the ocean.
He looks at me in disbelief,
And he says:
Nice arm…
And he breaks into a smile,
And that's when I know my mother's right.

We get married in September.

I dream of becoming a lawyer,
They're not smarter than me.
But then, I get pregnant.

The pregnancy is difficult—
The delivery is a blood bath.
I'll spare you the details.
Point is, the doctor tells me flat out:
This one is probably going to be it.

And so, you know how it goes—
How you used to be the protagonist
In the story of your life, and now someone else is…
How your biggest hopes and fears,
They are no longer about you…
That goes double for me.

The next fourteen years,
I'm the happiest woman in the world.
We are a tight family.
You may think we don't have much,
But I know I have *everything*.

Lawrence grows up healthy—a happy healthy boy,
And he has this spirit about him—
This hunger for life—

He wants to try everything, eat anything,
He's so fearless people always notice—
How he falls on his butt at the ice rink,
And he gets right back up,
How he can do handstands,
Which he learned in one day,
How he walks right over
To a big dog he never met before
And pats it on the head, no fear whatsoever
Even after the dog barks.

He's not the most diligent student
But he's smart, so he gets good grades anyway,
And he and Carl have this special bond—
Carl is still a big boy,
Still loves to play video games…
On weekends, they're at it first thing in the morning.
One day Carl apologizes for making so much noise,
And I say, it's okay—
I'm used to it by now—In fact, I say,
I love the sound of Supermario in the morning.
Carl laughs, I don't know why—
He says, come on…
You know what that sounded like—
I love the smell of Napalm in the morning
And I've no idea what he's talking about,
So he tells me about Apocalypse Now,
And then, *I love the sound of Supermario in the morning*
Becomes one of our running jokes
These things we tell each other at random times,
And we all crack up,
And everyone else thinks we're crazy,

And then, one day, Carl's heart gives out.

I know how that sounds.
Like I'm telling the story wrong
Like I skipped a part
But that's how it happens—

A bolt from the blue, no warning sign—
He kisses me in the morning,
And then I brush my teeth,
And the kiss is lost,
And he never comes back.

But I have Lawrence.
He keeps me going,
And truth be told,
It is an easy thing for me
To focus all of myself onto him.

And Lawrence is strong.
Doesn't take him long to become the man of the house.
Of course he decides he's gonna be a cop,
Like his father.
I don't even try to dissuade him.

On graduation day,
I don't think I ever saw Lawrence so proud.
And I don't need to see Carl
To know how proud *he* would have been.

Lawrence has big plans—
He's going to be a detective,
Or maybe the Bureau,
But for now, he loves being out on patrol
The people, the drama, the stories—
Every weekend he has a new one to tell me,
And it makes us feel closer to Carl, too—
We know what he would say,
What would make him laugh,
What would make him shake his head
And say, Man… What's wrong with people?

Lawrence is like his father, alright—
A ladies' man, like Carl used to say—
I guess these days you'd say a *player*,
But it's not like he toys with anyone's feelings,
He's just a big flirt, and—

Okay… I guess I'm making excuses.
But he swears he's a serial monogamist—
Only one girl at a time,
Though the turnover is pretty damn fast.
The silver lining is I've got no one to be jealous of,
Because Lawrence always has time for me.
And even when he moved out,
He made it a point to stay within twenty miles.

I see some other men now and then.
There's one—Brad…
I hate the name Brad.
He works in insurance.
Which is boring
But he loves food
And he's generally nice…
Anyway—

One night, Lawrence responds to a dispatch.
Domestic disturbance.
Lawrence walks to the door.
The man steps out.
There's blood on his shirt
And he's holding a gun
Lawrence tries to calm him down—
He's got the voice, and he's got the confidence,
He tells the man, We can figure this out,
Don't do something you're gonna regret.
Unfortunately, the man is drunk.
He fires his gun and runs off.
Fortunately, he's so drunk,
His aim isn't any good—
The bullet grazes Lawrence's upper arm.
There's no serious damage.
Lawrence walks inside
And finds the wife in a pool of blood.
He calls the medics.
He stops the bleeding until they get there.

He doesn't tell me a thing until the next day,
And doesn't even mention he got shot,
So I don't have a chance to freak out.

Eventually the man gets caught.
Lawrence gets a mention in the paper
And a commendation from the chief.
By then I've said something
About the danger of the job,
And how maybe he should think about other dreams.
But Lawrence shows me a letter from the wife,
And says:
Mom—*this is what I do it for.*

Nine months later,
I'm in line for groceries when I get a call.
I recognize the police station's number.
I leave my stuff on the conveyor belt,
And I step outside.

After a while a clerk comes out.
He asks me, You still want the groceries?
The words sound garbled.
It's like I'm underwater.
Like I'm on the other side of something.
The phone's still on.
Mrs Jackson?
Are you still there?

Losing Carl was hard, but deep inside I knew,
I *knew* I would survive it,
I would *outlive* it,
There was too much left to do—

This is different.

This is when time splits in half
There was a life before
And now there's *something else*—
It's not the same as life—
I can see it in his eyes—

The clerk's eyes—
He knows—
He can tell—
He can tell *I'm on the other side.*

This time, Death entered my house to stay
Walked right in, like some loathsome landlord
Who hangs his coat on the rack
Takes a seat
Lights up a cigar
And says:
Didn't you know?

This is *my* house.

GABRIEL: I turn eighteen right after the trial.
Go straight from jail to adult prison.

Officer says,
Take off your clothes.
Then he says:
Open your hands
Raise your arms
Open your mouth
Raise your tongue
Run your fingers through your hair
Turn your head to the left
To the right
Lower your hands
Lift your penis
Lift your scrotum.

Some don't understand that word.
They need to be told:
Lift your balls.

Then he says:
Turn around
Lift your foot

Wiggle your toes
Other foot
Bend over
Spread your cheeks
Cough twice.

I know I'm being inspected for contraband.
But there's more to it,
The word they use,
It actually tells you—
You're being *processed*
Transformed into state property
Another item in the warehouse.

Guards mostly treat you like dirt.
They think they have to establish dominance.
It's fucking Animal Planet shit.

Some inmates act friendly
Some keep their distance
You might think they're *un*-friendly
But the thing is,
Those guys offering you a smoke or a snack?
They're trying to get their hooks in.
And the one who mind their own business—
They're trying to give you some space.

I don't understand that.
I get a lot of stuff wrong.
I don't understand this place.
All I know is I'm a small fish in the shark tank
And I don't wanna make any bubbles.

Meanwhile, my brother's out.
Now it's his turn to come visit me.
He gives me some schooling.
He tells me,
You're young.
You're gonna get tested.
Don't let 'em get away with nothing.

Sure enough, one day someone steals my shit.
Doesn't even pretend he didn't.
So I know he's gonna do it again.
He's gonna steal from me what he wants,
And everybody's gonna do the same,
And stealing's just the beginning.
I'm about to become prey.

Later that day I get myself some batteries.
Stuff 'em in a sock and tie a knot.
Then with the sock I bash his head in.
That's how I get my first stay in the hole,
And I get my reputation.
That's the day I'm no longer an *inmate*.
Now I'm a fucking *convict*.

But I'm still facing life.
Can't go through this by myself.
So I start putting in work.
That means, you smuggle shit in
You pass messages out
You deal with those who need dealing with.
If the big homies say so,
You get your iron wet --
No punking out, no question, no argument,

Because,
Bottom line—
This isn't the free world.
In the free world
You're not expected to avenge
Someone you didn't even know
You don't have to take orders
From guys you never met
Guys locked up for life
Five hundreds miles away
In the free world
Violence is a last resort
Not the first response

People don't tattoo their faces
To advertise that they're killers.

'Course, putting in work
Will get you sent back to the hole.
Each time you'll end up in there longer.
23/7 alone in your cell
One hour in a dog run
Still alone
No yard time
No fresh air
No activities
Nothing

When you get back to population,
You're gonna have some issues.
You're gonna have, you know, *demons.*
Soon you get into more trouble,
Which gets you more time in the hole.

Eventually, they move me to another prison.
Pelican Bay. A supermax.
Set up for long-term solitary confinement
Out at the far edge of nowhere.

I'm twenty-seven.
The game has changed now.
I've been validated by I G I—
Institutional Gang Investigators.
That means I'm officially considered
Part of a Security Threat Group.
That means they will keep me in solitary
For the next six years
Before they even review my status.
Then all they gotta say
Is that they don't like my attitude --
I've been confrontational
Disrespectful
A pain in the ass

I threw up a gang sign
Made a gang-related drawing
I spoke a suspicious language—
Nahuatl if you're Mexican,
Swahili if you're black,
Gaelic if you're white
That's it:
Clock starts over.
There goes another six years.

Guards tell us there's three ways to leave this place:

Snitch
Parole
Die

My parole hearing is decades away.
No fucking way I'm gonna turn snitch,
And do my time in a PC yard.
That's not 'Politically Correct'—
It means Protective Custody,
Where they send snitches,
Rapists, child molesters and shit like that.
They call it protective,
But you can still be killed in there—
And anyway, even if no one gets to you
One day you might be back on the outs—
Good luck surviving
With a snitch jacket on.

So I know I'm gonna be stuck in this hole
With up to seven other men at a time
Four on the ground floor and four above
No one facing anyone
Just *stacked*
Like a bunch of fruit
With the rot spreading from one to the next.

This could be the rest of my life.

They say time is an illusion.
You know, relativity and all that.
But you still have to live inside it.
Inside that illusion.
Far as you can tell,
Time pulls days out of your future,
Stacks them up on the other side
Until, one day…
There's no more days left.
That's just the way it is.
Time does its thing,
You gotta roll with it.

Except some of us can't.

It's like we never sync up—
We were born too soon
Our parents were too young
We grew up too fast
We stayed up too late

Time was always off
Always a problem
Always the enemy
Time was our mom working nights
Late marks at school
Past-due notices
And cut-off services
Two-hour lines at the welfare office
Twenty seconds to outrun the cops

And then, finally,
Time becomes this whole other beast…

It becomes a *sentence*.

ANNA: I should know this from when Carl died,
But his mother handled it at the time.

So, the funeral director explains to me
That coffins and caskets aren't the same thing.
Coffins are tapered at the top and bottom,
Wider at the shoulders;
Caskets are rectangular.
He says that's what people tend to prefer.
That's why there's a better selection.
He says wood caskets are the most popular.
They come with brass handles and a name plate.
You can have decorations on the side panels,
Flower carvings, biblical inscriptions.
But then again, there are options.
Bamboo, wool, wicker,
Even recycled cardboard,
A hundred percent bio-degradable.

I see my reflection on the smooth polished wood
These boxes—
That's not—
That's not where he belongs
My son— *Where has he gone?*

I hold my breath until I can say:
Just a traditional one.
Thank you.
No decorations.
Just plain.

Thank you.

(A pause)

The killer's high on meth.
He drives his pale-blue Toyota truck
Right up to the front
Of a Chevron gas station off Highway 10.
He's not wearing a mask
So he's easily identified afterwards.

Soon as he's out the door,
The gas station clerk rings the cops.

Lawrence is six blocks away
So he responds to the dispatch.

The killer sees him and steps on the gas.
He drives straight at Lawrence, like a kamikaze.
Lawrence swerves.
The killer hits a parked van.
He gets out of his truck and starts firing his gun.
Lawrence gets out his cruiser to return fire

But he's shot in the throat
And he falls on the street
And then he's shot again.
Afterwards, no one will tell me
How long he stayed conscious
How long he suffered
How soon he knew he was going to die.

The killer is found two days later.
He's shacked up with a girlfriend.
Both have long criminal records,
Both are drug users,
Both are considered armed and dangerous.
But when the SWAT team breaks in,
They're both passed out in bed,
Like they have no care in the world.

Two hundred and forty-five dollars.
That's what the killer scored.

I drop twenty-five pounds.
I lose twenty percent of my hair.
I receive a hundred and fifty-six cards,
Which I stick inside two shoeboxes.
I'm forty-four years old.
I read somewhere that my life expectancy
Is another forty-two years.

Brad sticks around six more weeks,
Before he admits, this is more to deal with
Than he bargained for.

Forty-two years to go.

GABRIEL: I'm good with numbers.
Didn't get good grades in school,
'Cause…well, I didn't give a shit.
But I knew my grandma used to make
Twelve thousand dollar a year cleaning houses.
That was a grand a month.
My sister's drug habit was a gram a day.
A year of grandma's salary
would have lasted her four months.
One day of fucking got her three hundred bucks.

In solitary I start counting everything.
The days
The hours
Push ups sit-ups burpees
Three sets
Fifty reps per set
Two more sets
Twenty-five reps

My cell is seven by nine
I have seven by three to sleep
Two full steps take me wall to wall
Fourteen steps to the exercise cage
Fivesteps go wall to wall in the cage

4836 is how many holes
Are carved into my steel door.

In prison you get your own numbers.
Your alphanumerical I D.
It indicates when you went down.
Say it starts with a C,
Then I know it's about early Eighties.
If the C was an E
Then it might be the Nineties.
The system went through the As in about twenty years.
B took about a dozen.

C just half as long.
D lasted four.
E got used up in two.
It's like prison is this thing—
This machine that eats up life,
Faster and faster
Like that comic book villain,
Galactus
Devourer of worlds.

There's this older guy named Lloyd
He's in another pod
But we talk through the door between exercise cages.
Every day he works out in his cell
Before he even comes there,
Then meditates for two hours.
He likes to say,
Every heart is a clock.
A special clock,
With a set number of beats.
He says humans get two billion
Most animals get half that
Horses rabbits elephants whales
The beat count is similar
Though the life span is not.
That's because hearts beat at a different pace
The slower the beat, the longer you live.

I start thinking, maybe there's something to that.
You got 86,400 seconds per day.
So say you're a sedentary dude
With sixty beats a minute on your resting pulse.
Each day your heart beats 24/60/60
Which means 86,400 times.
Now, let's say you work out
You go an hour a day with a pulse of 160
Your resting pulse drops to 50
That means your heart beats 23/60/50

Plus that extra 160
That's only 78,600 times
Exercise saved you 7,800 beats a day
Every ten times you do it, you add a day to your life.
That's what Lloyd believes, anyway.

The tricky part is,
You want your heart to go slower
But you want the years to go faster.
Sooner or later something's gotta give.

Lloyd has a little daughter.
One day she gets run over by a truck.
Lloyd asks to attend the funeral.
Permit is denied.
Lloyd hangs himself.
Two days later they've got another dude in there.

ANNA: When we were children, my sister always said:
I can't wait.
Can't wait for my birthday,
Can't wait for Christmas,
Can't wait for spring break…

My mother would tell her, You should never say that.
When you hurry the future,
You're wishing your life away.
Don't do that.
Think of tomorrow, but live for today.
That's the only time you're really alive.

I knew what she meant.
I got it.
I lived in the moment.
I loved being my age, whatever that happened to be.
I was never in a rush to get older.
I never missed being younger.
I loved waking up early and watch the sun rise.
I loved to be ready for life.

There's that old expression—
Time stops.
It isn't quite like that. More like, time *changes*.
Suddenly, I don't understand it.
I can't estimate it.
Is it night?
Am I supposed to go to bed?
I can't boil an egg without checking the clock.
Has it been five minutes?
An hour?
People keep telling me to hang in there
Just put one foot in front of the other
Just keep moving forward
But what if you don't want to go forward
What if there's nothing for you there
What if you just want to go back?

And here's the other thing:
Tragedy makes you an outcast.

People say things like:
I'm here for you,
Anything you need,
And most of them don't mean it at all.
Here for you
Anything you need
That's just names they want to be called
Take 'em up on it, and they'll disappear.
There's sympathy for the grieving—
But it comes with an expiration date.

One day, I see Mrs Webb
Slinking behind an aisle at the grocery store.
Two weeks later, I catch myself doing the same.
Hiding from Mrs Webb,
To spare her the trouble to hide from me.

I become a shut-in.
I watch daytime television.

I try to read, but concentration's impossible.
I try to exercise but I have no strength at all.
Sometimes I go out, but I have nowhere to go.

And then one day, I'm just driving around, killing time
I'm halfway there
Before I realize where I'm really going
The Chevron gas station on Highway 10

The blood has been washed off
The chalk outline is gone
But I know exactly
I know *exactly* where it was
It's branded into my brain
It's carved into my soul

And something says *Do it*—
And I lay myself on the road.

(We hear a truck approaching. ANNA *doesn't move.)*

GABRIEL: When someone new comes to the hole
He's always an object of curiosity.
He's the week's best entertainment.
People yell questions from the other cells.
What's your name?
Where you from?
How long you looking at?
What's up in El Monte?
What's up in B Yard?
People need to know where the guy fits—
And they want news from the world outside.

But soon the questions fade.
It's hard to talk to people you can't see.
You have to yell, which is tiring,
And anyone can hear.
So, back to silence.
Back to boredom.

But to call it boredom…
It's really not the right word.
I don't know if there is a word.
It's not something.
It's a non-thing.
Empty time.

You think of your life as a story
But that's where the story ends
No more past present future
Story's over—Time is broken
You keep re-living yesterday
You've already lived tomorrow
It's like time just repeats
No change
No direction
No shape

You don't mark the calendar
To count down the days
You mark the calendar
So you know it's Monday
'Cause soon as you stop keeping track
You're gonna be lost in the desert
Drifting in the ocean
Stuck on the frozen mountain
Without a map or a compass
Or the fucking North Star.

"Serving time"—
Always found it a strange phrase
What is the service?
Time has no use for you
Time doesn't even know you

But in solitary, it gets worse
You're serving time
And now time has gone insane

Space breaks down, too
The cell becomes part of you
You mind-meld with it
The food slot becomes
Another body cavity
You get food in
Some guys throw shit out
I mean, actual shit

Long-distance vision falls apart
But hearing and smell become oversensitive
All day you smell other guys' feet
Their farts
Their bad breath
And the silence is torture
But the noise is worse
It can go off like a bomb
Banging
Howling
Screaming
And you can't stop it
You just start screaming back

Your head aches your stomach clamps your heart races
Your body turns against you
It's become another tool for punishment
This thing that can be shackled beaten frozen burned
Same for your mind
Becomes its own torture chamber
Just keeps filling with hatred
With fear
Nothing makes any sense
Nothing means anything
Day after day after day after day
Until you don't even know what the fuck a day is
You don't even know what *you* is
'Cause the only one talking to you is *still* you

You see the air crackling
The walls throbbing
You feel them pushing on you
You try to push back with your mind
Keep the walls away
But you feel like your brain
Is gonna be squeezed out of your ears

And prisons are haunted
Your cell has ghosts in it
Ghosts of those who came before
Who left behind their smells
Stains
Marks on the walls
Like graffiti in a cave

Ghosts of the people you hurt
Their dead eyes staring at you
Ghosts of women you knew
The ones you slept with
You fantasize about them so much
They become mythological creatures

The free world has boundaries
To keep ghosts away
Here, the ghosts spill over
The ghosts become real—and everybody real
Your friends
Your family
They all become ghosts

Eventually, you start wondering
If you've become a ghost, too
You can't really see yourself
Your cell doesn't have a mirror
You see your reflection in toilet water
Which is the only thing that can leave this place
You can flush and watch your reflection dissolve
And imagine it's escaping with that water

But you're still here
Neither alive nor dead
You start cutting yourself
To make sure you still bleed.

I write a letter to Ramon's mother.
She doesn't answer it.
So I talk to Ramon's ghost
And I tell him

I'm sorry

ANNA: My mother told me:
Aging means becoming lonely.
Your life narrows and narrows,
Until it comes down to your family,
And a small group of friends,
And then one by one your friends die.

At least it's supposed to be gradual.
So you have a chance to adjust.
To be graceful about it.

But murder—
Murder makes you alone at once.
And it doesn't just destroy the future.
Your past warps, too
It becomes a riddle,
A map of signs and clues
That you were too dumb to see before.
Everything you remember becomes an omen

All the feelings get twisted—
Like, I'm grateful that Carl died,
'Cause death spared him from this—
And then again I'm angry—
How could he let me face this alone?
And then I feel guilty,

For making this about me,
But there's no one to apologize to.

You find yourself doing strange things.
The kind of things you don't even want to tell anyone.
Listening to an old phone message—

Let me know if you need anything
I can get it on the way over

And for a moment—
A split second—
You can pretend he's coming home.

One day I'm in an elevator,
I get this familiar whiff of aftershave—
I fall apart on the spot—
And you don't want to explain that—
I'm sorry, Sir, your aftershave
Reminds me of my murdered son, Lawrence—

Easier to pretend you have an allergy—
Easier to pretend you're crazy.

But am I really pretending?

I've started seeing ghosts
Carl
Lawrence
Lawrence's killer—he's not dead yet, so maybe
That's not technically a ghost
He mostly shows up in my nightmares

And then, my own ghost…
The person I was.
The nest-builder.
The wife, the mother.
I can still see her, fluttering around the house,
Cooking dinner for her men.
Smiling
Like this is never going to end.

I tell the doctor I can't sleep.
I roll in my bed and soak the sheets in cold sweat.
The doctor prescribes Xanax for anxiety,
Ambien to sleep,
And Prozac for overall mood control.
He says the Xanax and Ambien will work day by day,
But Prozac is a long-term project.
You need to stick with it.
it requires commitment.

I have no commitment.
I'm not committed to my next breath.
I'm not even sure I want my mood controlled.
I don't want the pain, but pain is connected to memory,
And the memory I can't afford to lose—
I dread nothing more than waking up one day
Unable to recall my son's face.

But I don't leave home without Xanax.
Don't even try to sleep without Ambien.

I make a statement in court.
It's called an impact statement.
I address the killer. I say, *look at me.*
He doesn't.
I tell the jury about Lawrence.
I don't even cry. I'm too angry to cry
Though I notice some in the room do.
I explain that I used to have mixed feelings
About the whole death penalty thing.
That was *then.*

That was when I had a son.

GABRIEL: People in prison have drug problems.
That's why most are here in the first place.
Because they sold drugs bought drugs
Grew drugs stole drugs
Stole money to buy drugs.

Course, when you put 'em in prison,
They need their drugs even more.
Only way to forget where they are.
Inside, drugs are forbidden—
Which means that gangs control the supply.
Weed, crank, smack—you can get 'em
If you are willing to pay the price.

But In the hole, street drugs are hard to come by.
100 Mg of Thorazine?
They'll hand that out like candy.

Doctor comes to my cell, asks:
Do you have any problems?
Like I really wanna tell him there,
With all the other dudes listening.
So I don't tell him shit.
Fuck yeah, I got problems,
But I let them get worse and worse,
Until finally I *act out*
And the doctor puts me on a bunch of pills.
They work no better than weed,
But money goes to the right folks.

I make up a Pantheon
Bet that's a word you didn't think I knew
I imagine the drugs like ancient and terrible Gods,
Who travelled from Babylon to Aztlan.

The Gods of Anxiety—
Diazepam Alprazolam Bromazepam

The Gods of Depression—
Amitriptyline Paroxetine Mirtazapine

The Gods of Psychosis—
Risperidone Haloperidol Zuclopenthixol

And then, at last:
The Gods of Death.
These are the special drugs

That they use in the execution chambers.
Their names change from time to time,
'Cause prisons get what they can get
They must dodge all kinds of laws and restrictions—
Prisons are full of drug traffickers
But prisons *become* the drug traffickers
When they need drugs to kill you.

Mood-control meds, we call 'em bug juice
You know, for those who bug out
And people bug out *all the time*
They go viking—
A viking is a guy who stops washing—
They become shit artists
A shit artist is someone who harvests his feces
Sculpts them into objects
Paints the walls with them
A bungee-jumper is someone who hangs himself

I've known so many who lost their minds
The one who thought he was God
The one who thought he was the devil
The one who was a Civil War hero
The one with ninety-three children
All boys
All named Steve

The one who ripped all his nails off
Emilio
He started with the nails
Then cut up his arms
Then moved on to his legs—

Thing is, your body is not yours to harm
Harm yourself, you're gonna get punished
Just as if you're caught jacking off
But punishment only makes you crazier
So people harm themselves *more*
Smash their heads on the wall

Drink the detergent
Eat the lightbulbs
Wrap themselves in toilet paper
Then set the paper on fire

Eventually Emilio goes for an eye
Enucleates it
There's another ten-dollar word for you
He rips the optic nerve
Pulls out the bulb
Holds that shit in his hand
Looks at his eye
With his other eye

And then he eats it

I tell myself to hold on
Hold on to your sanity
You will not go crazy
You are not a ghost

One day a kite comes
From this guy who says he's a poet
I never asked to read his stuff
'Cause I don't wanna have to tell him it's bad
But now he's about to be moved, he needs surgery
So I tell him, hey—
send me a poem
I get the kite and I read:

This is my kingdom of pain
This is my valley of tears
This is the house of my rage
This is the pit of my fear
This is my silent scream
This is my poisoned heart
This is where love ends
This is the other part
This is where dreams bleed out
This is where madness springs

This is the tale it tells
This is the song it sings

ANNA: A year before Carl died,
He recovered some properties
Stolen from a doctor's house.
They had sentimental value, so the doctor told him,
Let me know how I can repay you—
I know it's your job, but I'd love to help if I can.
He was a fertility doctor,
So Carl asked him for a consultation.
The doctor said things had changed—
Now there were ways for us to have another baby.
He had my eggs and Carl's sperm frozen,
So we wouldn't have to rush a decision.

After Carl dies, I want to have that baby.
It would be the child of a dead man,
But I would love that child for both of us.

Before I call the doctor, I get a call from him.
Something about liquid nitrogen,
The thermometer stopped working,
And now all the eggs are dead and his sperm is gone.
I tell myself, it's alright. It wasn't meant to be.

After Lawrence is killed,
I wish I had that baby.
I feel ashamed to even think about it.
Of course, no one could replace Lawrence.
But these are the fake choices
The dead-end regrets
That slowly drive you crazy.

I fantasize about suicide.
I clasp the steering wheel
And imagine giving it a sharp pull,
The car slamming into the lamppost
And my brain switching off for good.

I stand on a rooftop and close my eyes
And I picture clear blue water below,
And my perfect dive.

I get serious about it.
I do the research.
Break down the components.
Time, Place, Instruments.

Helium. Tank, pipe, bag, elastic.
Painless. Fast. Clean. No danger to anyone else.
My place, two a.m. No chance of interruption.

I definitely want to be around for the execution.
Maybe wait for my parents to be gone first.
But there is comfort in knowing how I will do it.

One day, a friend mentions *forgiveness.*
Funny how people talk about it,
When they don't have to do it themselves.
Easy for them to think they would forgive.
To flatter themselves, thinking they're so enlightened.

Me, even if I wanted to—I simply could not.
Because I know that Carl wouldn't.
His parents won't, either.
For me to do it, it would be a betrayal.
And anyway: I don't want to.

Maybe that's not Christian of me.
Truth is, I don't think that much about God.
Way I figure, it's up to God to break the silence.
God gets no more credit at my store.
If God exists, God owes me an explanation.
God owes me a damn apology.

Maybe one day God will say to me:
I'm sorry... Forgive me for what I put you through...
And I will stare back
Into God's all-seeing eye
And I will tell him:

No
Let the angels look down at me in dismay—
No
Let God strike me dead on the spot—
NO

And if God says, you're right
I don't deserve forgiveness
I made you capable of so much love
And then let it turn into suffering
I made you capable to bear so much suffering
But I made you suffer *more*

I *broke you*, again and again and again—
It was just *wrong*
And I accept your anger
If God says *that*—

Then God and I can talk.

GABRIEL: I read every book in the prison
To keep my mind occupied.
It's mostly crap.
Paperback thrillers.
Romance novels.
But there are a few good ones.
Shakespeare.
Jack London.
Mark Twain.
I even read *Moby Dick*—
I struggle with it, but when I get it, I love it.
I start writing letters to schools.
Libraries.
Bookstores.
I ask them to send me more books.
And as I keep reading,
I start thinking harder about this place.

Society loves punishment
Crucifixion
Burning at the stake
Hanging
Electrocuting
Solitary confinement
But nothing like that ever stopped crime—
Think about it
Nothing like that ever stopped crime.
Makes you wonder, don't it?
How society keeps using
Something that's never worked.

And everybody knows it's not fair—
That if you're broke you get punished
And if you're rich you get off
That the darker the skin
The longer the sentence
That criminals aren't the same
And victims aren't the same, either—
Kill a black man,
It may get you life
Kill a white girl
It *will* get you death
Kill your wife
Life
Kill the bank manager
Death
kill another convict
Life
Kill a cop
Death

It's easy to put men away
Out of sight out of mind
Except it doesn't work out like that

I'll tell you what prison is:
Take all the things everybody fears

Poverty
Shame
Sickness
Violence
Death
Blend them together
Add ignorance
Hatred
Take away space
The final product is a special disease
It doesn't stay within the walls
It seeps into the ground
Goes home with the guards at night
Spreads through families
Neighborhoods
Cities
You know these places in the world
These places where something so bad happened
That even the names start sounding like a curse?
Auschwitz
Rwanda
Aleppo
Prisons are like that
All the names become toxic
Even the ones that would sound
Like vacation resorts
If you didn't know any better
Pelican Bay
Pleasant Valley

Or the ones that sound like a technical formula
A D X
Could be a diet supplement
A piece of exercise equipment
And they don't call this the hole,
They call it the SHU—
(Note: pronounced like "shoe")

Special Housing Unit
People get paid to make up this shit

And that's the whole point
Someone gets locked up
Someone else gets paid
It's not about fixing anything
your life is a commodity
A natural resource
Something to be *extracted*

And that's *the whole fucking point.*

ANNA: I heard it all.
All the what ifs,
All the buts,
All the excuses.
Hurt people hurt people.
Depraved 'cause he was deprived.
The impoverished childhood,
The absent father,
The early exposure to violence and drugs.

To which I say:
So what?
You don't choose the cards you're dealt
But how you play them— *That's on you.*

I worked in law offices.
I've been around police work, murder cases—
My whole life, even before Lawrence was killed.
I've seen defense lawyers celebrating
After getting a murderer off.
They knew he was guilty, the evidence was there—
But they were able to get it ruled out
Dismissed on technicalities
If you asked them how they lived with that,
They'd say, *The client's entitled to the best defense.*

Truth is, they get off on it.
Rubbing elbows with evil.
Makes 'em feel *special*.

I respect the law—but I don't respect them.
Defenders of serial killers
mass murderers
Sexual predators
The worse the crime, the nobler they feel
For defending the criminal.

They'll represent the man
Who strangled his six-year-old niece
With the Christmas lights
The one who shot his wife in the kitchen,
Right in front of their children,
And then set her on fire,
Leaving the kids to douse the flames
With their sippy cups

And then there was the man
Who was calmly watching T V
When the police came to the house
And found his baby in a closet, hanging upside down,
With his mouth sewn shut
Because the man was sick of the crying
The autopsy found snapped ribs
Burn marks from cigarettes
And ligature marks on the penis to block urination.

These are true stories.

They say the death penalty is inhumane
It's irrational
If killing is wrong, don't kill a killer to prove it

I have a different take
I've come to another conclusion
Men kill
That's just a fact

Lizard kills bug
Rat kills lizard
Bird kills rat
But men—
Is there anything that men *don't* kill?
Fish
Fowl
Cattle
Wild beasts
Strangers
Family
Ourselves
The planet
Jesus Christ our Lord—

And civilization only made it easier—
From stone to arrow
From arrow to bullet
From bullet to missile—
Civilization is another name for striking distance.

Truth is, men will do *anything*—
Anything at all—
If they think for a minute
That they'll get away with it.
Impunity is the mother of horror.

Finally the day comes.
The Police Officers Association has chartered a bus,
But they drive me there in a private car.

There are eleven other witnesses.
There is a one-way glass separating us from the
execution chamber.

At six P M the killer gets wheeled in.
He raises his head.
He looks straight at me.
I know he can't see me
But I wish he could.

I wish he could see my eyes,
And know there's no pity there.

He mumbles something I don't quite hear
Sounds like a half-hearted cuss
Then the drugs are released into the IV.
After a while he groans.
Takes a few deep breaths, then a few shallow ones.
His eyes close, and he stops moving
Like he went to sleep,
Nice and easy,
And I can't help thinking:
That's it?

For a moment he comes awake again,
And he lets out a little yelp,
And then the execution team pulls the curtain closed.
We sit there for another half hour.
We hear people walking in and out,
Until finally, someone tells us it's over.
Someone whispers to me,
Congratulations.

After the execution, I learn about the killer's last meal.

Steak burritos
Grilled shrimp
Black beans
Baked potato with butter
Coca Cola—a six pack—
Pepperoni pizza
Ice cream
Chocolate and vanilla

I am offended by it.
His appetite.
His gluttony.
And I'm offended by the fact that it was indulged.

The prison showed him compassion.
Lawrence didn't get any.
He didn't get to pick his last meal.

(A pause)

Closure is a myth.
I feel no better.
I sleep no better.
I'm the lost sailor on a raft
Who gulped down the salt water
And now is thirstier.

I'm going to leave the great state of Texas—
I'm moving to California, next to my sister.
No—I'm not chasing a new beginning
I'm just changing the scenery before the end.

GABRIEL: Four bread slices
Two cheese slices
Two processed meat slices
One fruit
Six carrot sticks
Six celery sticks
Cup-size milk carton
Two cookies
That's your standard meal
Unless you leave your food
Complain
Misbehave
And then you get the loaf.

The loaf is:
Chopped bread
Imitation cheddar
Canned spinach
Canned beans
Potato flakes
Tomato paste

Powdered milk
Spoiled cabbage optional
Spit on it at will
Mix until stiff and bake in the oven.
Final product should be chewy and unpleasant,
And make you think of shit.

When you get the loaf,
You better eat the loaf.
Turn down the loaf,
You gonna keep getting the loaf.

Until you reach the point
Where you go, *fuck it*
I'm done
I'll torture my own self.
If I can't control nothing
I will control *that*.

We go on a hunger strike.
It fizzles out.
We do it again.
And then again the next year.
This time it's *big*—thousands of people,
All over the state.

The first few days you don't eat
Your body runs on glucose reserves.
Then it goes into ketosis
And starts to use up body fat.
After three weeks
It starts on muscles and organs
You're eating yourself alive
You can feel your insides shrivel
You brain runs out of power—
But we keep going.

The warden has an idea.
We're a few days from July the 4th,
So he announces a special holiday menu.

Hamburgers
Hot dogs
Taters
Coleslaw
Salad
Ice cream
And
Strawberry shortcake.

Some of us haven't seen a strawberry
In twenty fucking years.

When the meal cart comes around
The smell is overpowering
I never thought I'd hear grown men cry over
strawberry shortcake
Now I'm one of those men
I stick my head into the toilet
So I can smell shit instead.

But we keep going.

Somehow
In the ruins of our lives
Something has been created
Built instead of broken
Our dignity has become stronger
It's become *adamant*, and immense
And we' re all willing to die for it
Tomorrow
Today
Right now
Singing all the way through
And none of us has seen this before
All the races together
Guys who woulda killed each other on sight
Gang politics, race wars—
Finally none of it matters
One race

The prisoner race
One enemy
The prison system
And they can bring more chains
Build more walls
Our bodies will die
But our souls will be free—
Free in this world
Or free *from* it.

The strike becomes big news.
Radio, press, T V
First local, then national.
There's more strikes all around the country.
Prison authorities start negotiating.

For once, we win the fight
The system will be reformed
And most of us in solitary
Get to go back to population.

I get transferred to a new prison.
This warden has new ideas.
I start programming—
That's prison lingo for things like job training
Anger management
Drug rehab

They bring in motivational speakers
Successful businessmen
Talking about success.
Most criminals are capitalists.
They eat this stuff up.

One of the speakers is kind of obnoxious.
White guy
M B A
He's got expensive clothes
And a cheap rap about responsibility.

I keep my face neutral
But in my mind I'm thinking

You don't know who I am
You don't know where I'm from
You're from a good home
Meals cooked on a stove
You didn't eat out of a bag
Your shoes never had holes
Your parents took you to the doctor
That doctor knew your name

I'm from a different world
Apartments rented by the room
Needles on the sidewalk
Vomit on the steps
Death threats on the wall
Your father bought you a car
Mine left me a three-inch scar

So fuck you and your life lessons
For a life I'll never have.

But I don't want any trouble.
So I keep my mouth shut.
Can't let them know.
Can't let them see the rage.

ANNA: In California, I start working as a notary,
And a private student tutor.
It's nice to be unknown.
To be able to share only as much as I want.
But there's this bleeding-heart liberal—
Lots of them around here—
Her name is Alycia
She volunteers for a nonprofit.
Somehow she learns all about me
And she invites me to speak at a prison event.

She wants me share the victim's perspective.
She tells me about *restorative justice*.

I don't believe in it.
Justice is justice.
Doesn't need any qualifiers.
There's nothing to restore,
Unless you can raise the dead.

I say I'm probably not the right person.
But she says I can be honest about my feelings
The inmates can take it.
They need to hear it.

Two days later, a neighbor is carjacked at gunpoint.

I'm at a dinner party with this guy Todd.
I've already been out with him twice.
Of course, nothing happened.
He doesn't know how lucky he is.

I had sex a bunch of times in the last ten years.
You may say it's been touch and go.
Sometimes I have to get drunk first.
Sometimes I freeze in the middle of it.
Sometimes I want so bad to lose myself
That I want to get hurt—
And one time, I end up hurting the guy...

Anyway—Todd doesn't know any of that.
He just expects some fun and games.
I can tell he's getting frustrated.

Someone brings up the carjacking.
Todd starts spouting liberal platitudes.
I have a feeling he wants to provoke me.
This other couple agrees --
Socioeconomic blah blah
Child neglect blah blah blah
Education blah blah blah blah

They don't know my history
So they lay it on thick

I say, *Come on*
Stop making excuses
For bullies who beat up kids to steal their sneakers
Self-proclaimed thugs who call women hos and bitches
Psychotic assholes who dream nothing better
Than living in a rap video—

There once was a man
Whose father whipped him until he was fifteen
He was harassed beaten jailed
Not for any crime but for what he believed
That man was Dr Martin Luther King

So I'm not gonna feel sorry
For guys who waste their lives hurting others—

And to be honest with you,
I've had it with the hypocrisy—
You want social justice
But you want private schools
You want open borders
But you want gated communities
You want low carbon emissions
But you want to fly business class
You want to save the dolphins
But you want sushi for dinner
You want women's rights
But you want internet porn
You want to help the homeless
But you want them to stop hustling you
You want fewer cops
But you want them to show up fast—

And if someone even tries to point out the problem
You call it *complexity*
You think it makes you *interesting*—

I mean, seriously
Seriously
Give Me A Fucking Break!

The table freezes.
Todd says, Jesus.
No wonder you're still *single*.
I say Todd, honey, I'm not single—
I'm just married to a dead man.

I should call off this prison thing.
What the hell would I tell these guys?
Fuck it—they said I can speak my mind.
They asked for it.

GABRIEL: I keep programming.
Take more classes
Hear more speakers
And then I'm asked
Would I like to attend a special event.
Wives and mothers of murder victims,
Coming to talk about their experience.

I know they mean well.
But do I really want to hear it?
They only speak for themselves, anyway.
They don't speak for society.
They don't speak for Ramon's mother.
She wishes me nothing but death.

Still—
it's not like my calendar's full.
It's either that,
Or work out with a bunch of maniacs
Listen to some bullshit I heard before
And pretend I don't care
When the mail cart passes me by.

That day, we gather in the gym.
Prisoners in the middle
Guards around the perimeter
Speakers on the stage.
Mothers and wives.
They look at us.
Many of us have murder convictions.
We didn't kill their loved ones.
But we could have.

When the first mother starts talking,
She starts to cry,
And some of us are right behind.

The third mother is introduced.
Anna Jackson.
Wait.
Wait wait wait
My head starts spinning
I know that name

The first two mothers talked about healing,
Compassion
Anna Jackson—
Oh, she's different
She's got this *rage*
She speaks softly
But it's right there at the surface
It shoots out sparks like a live wire.

I think about my brother—Ivan
Such a magnet for trouble
He never learned to back down
I flash back to this one time
I was jailed for loitering on Halloween
I had this lame-ass Lucha Libre costume on
Two days later I'm released
Ivan picks me up
It's late in the morning

And here's this little thug
In torn red spandex
Taking the walk of shame
'Course on our way home
These guys start picking on me
Mira este puto
Who the fuck you s'posed to be?
Es El Perrito Chueco

Ivan tells them to shut the fuck up
There's five of them
All bigger than us
Ivan takes a beating
But he makes sure I don't
And when it's over
He spits blood right at the biggest guy's face—
Coolest thing I've ever seen.

After I go to prison,
Ivan's arrested a few more times.
Burglary
Weed
Assault
The usual gang shit

He moves out of state,
Bounces around a while,
Meets this woman in Texas
And moves into her double wide.
She's got serious drug habit
And he's got to tick the box—
The felony box on a job application
You can do the math
He ends up robbing drug dealers
Drugstores
Gas stations

One day he's caught in the act
He shoots his way out and kills a cop

Buys himself one more day
Before he's found and locked up.

He's sentenced to death
Decides not to appeal—
He doesn't find a life sentence
Any more attractive than early check-out.
I don't try to change his mind
I just write him to say that I love him
And I hope we will meet again.

After he's executed,
My sister comes to visit me
I haven't seen her in two years
But she attended the execution
And talked to people afterwards
So she gives me the play-by-play.

Ivan orders a large meal
He was always hungry
But this time, the appetite never comes
Ivan asks to send the meal
To some other guys on the row
Warden says nope
They don't get no special meal
Until it's *their* last meal

Ivan is driven to Huntsville
He speaks to a priest
He tells him, I'm not sure about God
Seen too many people get fooled
Pray for rain
And they get fire
Pray for parole
And they get life
Pray for death
And they're still here
So I'm not asking God for nothing
I'm just telling you what's in my heart.

He apologizes for his sins
And the priest tells him that God is waiting.
While that God waits
Three other Gods clock in
Midazolam
Vecuronium
Potassium chloride
One to put him to sleep
One to stop his breath
One to stop his heart.

Ivan is strapped to the gurney
He's wheeled into the chamber
They ask if he has any last words
He says: *Peace out.*

The needle man picks a vein
Ivan twitches
Midazolam enters his blood
Ivan falls asleep
Vecuronium descends
Then Potassium follows
And then…

Ivan wakes up.
He starts thrashing—
Turns out the vein collapsed
And the drugs leaked out
There's no more drugs left
But they don't try to save him either
That would defeat the purpose
So they watch him foam at the mouth
And thrash in that gurney
He's going through a series of strokes
And they just stand there, and watch
Until my brother's heart bursts.

I hear Anna Jackson talk.
I think about introducing myself

Then I think again
The prison made a mistake
We weren't supposed to be in the same room
But my last name is different than Ivan's
And prison bureaucracy is a mess.
If I told her now who I am
The prison would find out
And that would be the end of that
I decide to write her instead
I know she may never get the letter
But at least I can say what I got to say

*(Silent scene—*ANNA*)*

*(*ANNA *reads* GABRIEL's *letter. Puts it down. Picks it up.*
Puts it down again. Paces the kitchen. Finally she starts
writing. Stops. Crumples the paper. New page. Starts over)

*(Silent scene—*GABRIEL*)*

*(*GABRIEL *reads* ANNA's *letter. Starts writing)*

ANNA: *(Reading)*
Dear Mrs Jackson,
Thank you for your letter
It was a surprise to receive it
After shouting into the void
For so many years

In answer to what you said:
I do not expect you
To stop hating my brother
I will never fully understand
The enormity of your loss
You are right that he had many years to apologize
But he was like a malnourished pit-bull
Who only learned to fight

Honestly, I think he was afraid
Afraid to ask for forgiveness
Afraid to hear that he would be hated forever
Afraid to shed his armor of anger

I make no excuses for him
What he did cannot be excused
My own actions can't, either
But believe me when I say
That I would do anything to take them back

Please write back if you'd like to
It brightened my day to read your letter
Heated as it rightly was.
Sincerely,
Gabriel Jessie Wayland

GABRIEL: *(Reading)*
Dear Mr Wayland,
Your wish may well be sincere
But the hard truth remains
The bell cannot be unrung
The gun cannot be unfired
Some wounds cannot be healed
I have been raging into the void myself
Well over a decade now
I've pushed away all my friends, all my family
And still, the grief doesn't end
You may escape for a moment, a day,
And then it whispers in your ear:
Where have you been? We're not done
We are never gonna be done

ANNA: *(Reading)*
Dear Mrs Jackson,
Thank you for your honesty
I hear what you're saying

He was made of you
And my brother took him from you
I'm grateful that you're even able
To share your pain with me
I hold it in great respect

People tend to look away from pain
It frightens them, embarrasses them
But when you live like I do
You become attuned to it
You pick up the signal from the dawn of time
I cannot heal it
But I *hear* it
I feel it
I *honor* it

(Puts letter down)

It's as if someone
A faceless, soundless someone
Started listening...

he hears me

GABRIEL: She says that I'm a good writer
In my letters, she could see my heart
She says it's a good heart
And I know this
I believe this...
But I've never had anyone tell me

ANNA: I realize: we're *connected*
Related by blood
Spilled blood
The bond has no name
But it's permanent
It's irrevocable

There is an underground river
We live above it
But one day we fall
Sooner or later
For a day or ten years
We all fall into that river
And we may feel alone
But there's other people there

GABRIEL: There's always other people

ANNA: We just need to look
Just need to get used to the dark
And see

GABRIEL: And now she's going to do something
For me—
Something I didn't ask
Didn't even imagine
But she did—she thought of it—
She's going to speak to Ramon's mother

ANNA: And maybe that's the secret
It isn't *love*...
Love connects us selectively, one by one,
But *pain*... Pain is the underground river
Pain connects us all

GABRIEL: Ramon's mother writes me her own letter
She says she still hurts every day
But she doesn't hate me anymore
She accepts my apology
She doesn't hate me anymore

ANNA: He asks me to come visit.
And it occurs to me,
Last time I was eager to visit a prison
I went to watch his brother die

GABRIEL: There's a new law now—
An earlier shot at parole
If you committed your crime as a youth
It's still years away for me
I don't even know how I'd fit back in
I've never paid a bill
Never owned a computer
Haven't been touched by a woman in years
I don't know how to deal with people
I don't know how to *look* at people
I'm a convict
A felon

A gangster
A killer
But I've been called a new word

Forgiven

I feed on it

I am not a ghost

ANNA: Before I go visit, I have this idea
Something I haven't done in a long, long time
I call the warden about it—Warden says, no way
But I don't take no for an answer
And he finally relents
He will make a one-off concession.

See, Gabriel's birthday is coming up
I only know because I asked
And so...

(She opens the fridge, takes out a box...)

I've made a cake

It's just something I had to do
Thing is, Gabriel sent me a picture—
He wanted me to know what he looks like
Before we meet in person

He smiles—
In the picture—
And I wasn't prepared for that
I was not prepared at all...

How much he reminds me of them

(ANNA *and* GABRIEL *turn toward each other.)*

END OF PLAY

NOTE

In staged readings of the play, a small variation is suggested.

Gabriel's page 61 line "I decide to write her instead" should be followed by:
"She writes back, and I write again".

From that point, omitting the silent scenes, both characters should read their own words, rather than each other's.

www.ingramcontent.com/pod-product-compliance
Lightning Source LLC
Chambersburg PA
CBHW052218090426
42741CB00010B/2584